FORLORN LIGHT

Also by Nazifa Islam:

Searching for a Pulse, Whitepoint Press, 2013.

Nazifa Islam

FORLORN LIGHT

Virginia Woolf Found Poems

Shearsman Books

First published in the United Kingdom in 2021 by
Shearsman Books Ltd
PO Box 4239
Swindon
SN3 9FN

Shearsman Books Ltd Registered Office
30–31 St. James Place, Mangotsfield, Bristol BS16 9JB
(this address not for correspondence)

www.shearsman.com

ISBN 978-1-84861-784-1

Contents

I

II

III

I used only the words from individual paragraphs of Virginia Woolf novels to write each of these poems. I did not allow myself to repeat words, add words, or edit the language in each paragraph for tense or any other consideration.

"How can we combine the old words in new orders so that they survive, so that they create beauty, so that they tell the truth?"
—Virginia Woolf

for Abbu

I

Phantom Weight
The Waves

I exist to tremble in shriveled solitude
to burst into tears, to want.

Something in me—something made
of pine-needles, thunder, and grass—
has been torn out.

My crippled hands take whole days and crack them open:
morning hours slip out, unfurl
and I swallow time like it will give me wings.

In that moment, I see all of my restrictions—
they spring up and stand there
to be admired.

I want to be given freedom;
I want to unfold and fly.

The Middle of Alone

The Waves

I wake in the night glutted with penance
and ask *Will I break in half?*
Do I want someone to endure time for?

I am multitudes of people
but I have not loved suffering
and I grow numb

when the minutes are
yawning at me.

I long to laugh. Someone, remember
my scratched heart
with ease not anguish.

I am exhausted
with myself.

The Plunge Back

Mrs. Dalloway

She was eighteen. It was early
morning and she was standing on the terrace

looking at rooks rising into the air. She was musing
about flowers, about trees and vanished smoke

when a lark burst in the open window
like a winding wave and she forgot her calm.

Then there was the feeling
that something utterly awful had to happen—

and she remembered
that June. Solemn eyes, a chill

smile, a dull pocket-knife, his sharp kiss.
How strange. How like falling.

Only Her

Mrs. Dalloway

She was strange—a presentiment
of something
completely reckless—but her charm!

She sprang between disinterested
and protective

was bound to catastrophe
to idiotic bravado.

She did the most absurd things
was completely
overpowering and so she had

a sense of purity—spoke always of integrity
of chivalry
of being in league together.

She was not a
grown up.

Fixed on Her

Mrs. Dalloway

Her laughing eyes were gathered moonlight—
perfect yet mad. Infernally wild

all enraged instinct and disturbed courage
like cold water in Hell

she spoke to the wood and lake
cut flowers and people and meant them to hurt.

He had a feeling she suffered—
went out and cried alone—

but he never saw it.
After seeing her he began talking to the moon.

He would have done anything
for her. He wanted her.

Rid of Effulgence
The Waves

I see the moon—flickering, broken
leaning against
the sky—and am afraid.

I am a girl among men and women
robed in beauty but
without faces. Their tongues

cut; I am derided. Is there an end
to these knives? I lie
I stammer, I am on the verge
of twitching.

I am composed of scorched sea
foam and fire.
I am like a ribbon of weed.

When will I be
flung to the uttermost
corner of the world?

Like She Asked for Anguish

Mrs. Dalloway

Day in and day out
he gave her heartless grief

destroyed her independence
ruined everything he could.

It should have been intolerable
but how she cared for him!

She was convinced
he was her whole life.

And so he—the cold arrow in her
heart—was happy

and they married in a garden
where he told her

she was a silly flimsy thing
a failure, and all his.

Great Indifference
The Waves

You see me inarticulate and lost
shuffling sinister phrases
on note-paper.

You long for words but you see
I am broken and tattered.

You tell me that it has been a grey
stormy day
but the towering clouds
are changing now to trailing wisps.

You tell me true stories
of childhood triumph and love.

You seek the undeniably
beautiful.

How tired I am
of language and lovers.

Certainty

The Waves

People watching me see nothingness.
I am nameless. I choke

on the unknown, hoard gold amulets
looking-glasses, faces. I wonder

at admiration; I do not have
distinction or friends. I choose to hate—

to attach myself to violence
and disaster. I sit alone on the edge

of the world—imagine
the extraordinary, the immaculate—

and despise myself. I know
I should fall.

The Mind Arches
The Waves

Struck by a cold and violent god
I am blurred edges moaning at my own sense
of absurdity.
The door to chaos is open

and there is nobody to offer me understanding
here. I walk alone
but I need someone to talk to.

I—a bit of pitch and string and steam—
need a sympathetic figure
to come to me.

I feel the urgency of my solitude;
my story is poised
to disappear.

Ruined

Mrs. Dalloway

They met in the garden an angry morning
and right then and there

she was convinced he was everything
she had never asked for.

He was a horror—perfectly heartless.
He gave her cold pity and intolerable grief.

He called her a failure of a woman
a silly pretty prude.

He was never happy with her
and she never could understand him—

but still she cared
still she would find herself arguing with him.

Her whole life with him came
to assured anguish.

Her Instinct

The Waves

She stands among the stealthy and assured
in a corner of the barnyard.
There is no light. Dressed as a beast—
a bird's beak nailed to her
speared by the sharp moment—
her face assumes a dazed futility.
She is a wild creature now.
And yet—the alarming wish to be loved.

Doubt

Mrs. Dalloway

On the surface, he was positively charming—
he was graceful
and he seemed to radiate a silver love.

But over time he hurt her. With quarrels
and smugness
with scissors and his clenched fist.
He put her down.

He said he thought she was ordinary
that she was like a knife—cold and slender—
just not valuable.

If only she would swear at him!
Would detest him!
But while she thought their affair a failure
all she wanted was to save him.

Ourselves

Mrs. Dalloway

She caught green flowers for him
would tell him stories
under the fern tree, but he only frowned

and said the world was wicked—
the yellow grass, the city, the people
who chattered and laughed.

She said people fascinated her—the quiet stranger
on the bus, the man dead in the river—
they were all something

nice and odd. And suddenly
he saw her perfectly. He knew her. He felt her.
She was like the man killing himself

in the middle of the street.
She was happy.

The Playing-Field
The Waves

He walks across the field
like forlorn light

his magnificence
behind him.

Sheep settle on the rough grass.
The two great elm trees

despise him.
One slovenly cricket

is trooping clumsily
after his long stride

and his heart
is now heavy and yellow.

The wake of a battle
seems to lie

on the long grasses.
This is where

he will die—
he will choose

to buckle.

Another Day
The Waves

I feel the bruised cry of birds in my body
when I wake.

Thinness rushes my pink imperfect heart
 and I am cast down at another day—

hands and feet and body.
Here is idleness, brown water, disgrace.

The sun is yellow and laughing
leaves stir and patter across the lawn

and I long for darkness and sleep—
its brass thud, its pirouetting slam.

I lie here and watch the bedroom
harden into night.

Never Eternally
Mrs. Dalloway

The morning they parted he scolded her
for having the pink makings of poetry in her.
He calmly told her he saw

the state of her soul—all the defects—
and that however beautiful she might be
the world would never reward her

for it. How she argued—how she cared!
But over her he said
perhaps she was the perfect little girl

with his fine old bitterness
and suddenly
she cried.

Brim and Break

The Waves

My mother knits moths
in the evening.

Those insects grow pale
and full

like white flowers
and set on me—a pursuit.

I am hems, pinafores, socks
and hard eyes

in the grass.
I am still. A child

I desire
one thing: to love.

Collisions

The Waves

I cannot escape from damaged sleep
from endless dreaming:

I am suspended over waves.
My yellow wings cannot spread and so I fall;

I am alone with the hopeless desire to rise. I fold
up. I sink under darkness
am tumbled and turned. My body is soft

my mind frail. I am
travelling among black waves.

Is there earth above me?
Will I awake?

Presence

The Waves

He is gone. The fine filament
that spun between us

is darkened now. How strange
this moment. How alien.

He is returning to the world—
to that comfortable

simplicity—and I stand
in the lengthening flocking dark.

Spirits and familiars
are in the corners and the air

is mocking. I feel old.
I feel shabby. Who am I now?

My love took refuge
from me.

While I Breathe
The Waves

Even now, I am carrying you with me—your words
knotted in my handkerchief
your rage screwed up in a knife. I saw you
so unhappy. I followed as you passed out the door.
You heard me cry. You asked to be free.
You are always on my mind—a beetle
moving in the depths. Like a light
I waver. Will I go out?

Remembered

Mrs. Dalloway

Like the striking sound of a bell
his voice—vigorous, extraordinarily
alive—finds her in this room

and she is ill, she is falling.
Something in the recesses of her heart
holds grief years old.

He is her past. He is intimacy dead
and gone. For her, he was moment after moment

of sudden delight.
He was her clear unending future.

A tremor of suffering
buries itself in her.

The reluctant recollection of being
profoundly happy.

I Know Permanence
The Waves

I am feeling a sense of infinite darkness
of unlighted sky and time.

I call for golden light but not a flicker
crowns this avenue I walk down.
It has gone.

My brain seems a strip of cloud
my mind streaming with sudden random abysses
one following another.

What can I do? I have lost
my grip on the past
on feeling light.

How strange, this poem
how whirling.

There Was No Relief

Mrs. Dalloway

Daylight faded into a night
robbed of all colour.

Mist wound over the houses
and hillsides.

She huddled in the bleak dark
and cried. He was gone

and so she was turning mad.
By midnight

she was talking aloud
to the rivers, to the fields

to nobody—
I am alone! I am alone!

Her words were lost
in the blank darkness.

Would night never surrender
to the sparks of dawn?

Other People

The Waves

My face is heavy and angry
in the looking-glass—

people are laughing at it.
I duck and hide but I am seen

in a second. They say
they really know me.

They say I shift and change
when spoken to.

They are really here
but am I?

I look to the world
for what is real.

It laughs.

Us

The Waves

The elm tree in the park where I finally clutched your hand.
The rose umbrella I bought us.
Your voice.

I was so myself—opened up, stupid
always talking. Buzz, buzz, buzz.

You—faithless and empty—darted in and left me
battered and hollow.
Was I the wind of death to you?

When I knew our partings were forever
I walked my cut heart
down into the desert for a lion to destroy.

You once seemed tender.
I doubt it all now.

Where They Sat

Mrs. Dalloway

He left her years ago. He had expressed
being with her as unending suffering

so his coming back
in this moment is puzzling

and her voice is not laden with honey.
He had been her future.

He was delight itself.
A reluctant intimacy—in recollection

of the past—glides into her heart
yet she wants him gone. He was the one

she remembered
when the clock tolled the hour.

She had been extraordinarily happy.
Her grief is alive.

II

Without Sanctuary
The Waves

I saw him fall. His body suddenly twisted—
dangled for a moment
in time and space—then crashed and he went

into that strange solitude, that lightness, that unreality.
I saw Death pounce
and now my memory is torturing me.

I realize beauty is not freedom. There is no escape
from pain and the devils of grief
claw at all men. I know
happiness is a make-believe.

The lily withers, sparrows are driven out
of their orange trees, and a child in tears cries out
Will it never be morning?

Something Is Wrong
The Waves

It is winter and the past seems to speak—
voices in the dark sob lamentations.

I follow sunset paths that intersect and twist.
Trembling branches fall and point
and marvel over me.

I brush at a spray of stars—the filaments
infinitely fine.
My mind is akimbo.

I break damp books in careless hands
and spin in the indifference
of this night.

Put Out

The Waves

The world knocks hours on my bed—
they drop down green and quivering. They grow.
They ask questions I cannot
interrupt. Here I lie
hours suspended through my head.
Somebody, let the light in.

Before the Wave
The Waves

I float on a raft green with creepers
my freedom gone.

I drop brown petals and hollyhocks and a stone
into the icy waves.
The gale barks.

The waves rise and curl. Ships dash
against the cliffs
and the sea is red. A drowning sailor

reaches for the shore—
bubbles rise from the depths.

I rock side to side. My time is short.
I see the fallen lighthouse.
I have foundered.

In the Schoolroom
The Waves

Her body is thyme and chalk
her mind a white emptiness.
A butterfly circles her as she stares
at the blackboard
and pinching fear lodges in her back
in her shoulder-blades.
She has no story, no meaning
here. She has no wings.

She Admired the Dark

Mrs. Dalloway

She hadn't beauty and knew it.
Hour after hour of life came to stay and made her

feel cut to such an extent that she wrapped herself
in brown paper. The blood that rushed in her

veins shocked her. In summer she sat smoking after dinner
with her arms round her knees

talking to the floor. Society was not to be envied.
The world was nothing kind.

She could quarrel with literally anything:
the penny in her pocket

an old man talking to a ruby ring
the cows in the field. She liked nothing but evening

and night—where ideas were
when a private letter could be written.

Large-eyed life was always
upsetting her.

Remorselessly
The Waves

A terrible night—
the soundless dark
palpitating

shadow catching
on my flanks and fear moving
through me.

I am like a trembling
young animal.
I cower.

I hear the sigh
of the churning dead
and run.

I prepare to fall.
I seek some shelter
but I am

whimpering
in vain—
no one is coming.

The Bird in My Heart Was Frightened

The Waves

I ran like thrown light over the fixed earth
my legs quivering, my heart moving faster and faster.
I ran over pink geraniums. I saw green leaves
ripple on a still branch. I dashed past
the nest in the hedge with its dead bird and mould.
I cried and went on running.
I thought of nothing but moving, moving.

To Cease Completely
Mrs. Dalloway

Life was walking in front of her.
It was inevitably ugly—fat and plodding
and furious she had somehow survived
winter's white rages.

She knew fear was not her only
gift once. She had
branches and trees and the rambling
heat of the country sun once.

She remembered driving in dawn
mist, walking in the park, dancing
all night, being loved.

But now she was throwing
dreaming to the streets.
She was all bits and pieces.

Death looked at her
and purred.

What I Found

The Waves

I found a dead man by the apple trees
last night. His throat was cut;
he was floating in blood.

The silver moon glared down on us
from the pale-grey sky
and the clouds were white as dead codfish.

Standing in the implacable solitude
I felt sick and doomed
and all too delicate.

I was fixed to the leaves. I was tired.
I was unable to recover.
This was my hour of death.

Deep Ground

The Waves

I bury pretend scales
a shiny pebble, clear stones.

I bury winter and the dining-room.
I bury images
of lumps of meat.

I bury the red-brown cherry
and the whole attic.

I bury scattered hills
flat grass
all of the trees.

I bury ugly games and long
pitch nights. Home alone

I hear waves
booming. There are some
things to save.

Pirouetting

The Waves

I am red like clean decisive heat
like blown veins
streaking white cheeks.

I lap up cups of sweet hot milk
my eyes silver
in the kissed steam.

Even afraid of the crack
in the frozen earth
of hard people, of blind anguish

I am seized
with dancing dreams
of sunshine.

I am now as soft as
a green winter.

To Clasp Flowers
The Waves

My garland of deep green anguish
jerks at me and the pain is incandescent—

it is a knot of moonlight
and unsealed light.

It flows through my body
and leaves me trembling. Papery thin

and shivering I go into a book of flowers.
I wander by a passage

about cowbind on the river's edge
and my faint being is solid and warm

again. My body is now water-lilies
ivy, roses. I am not

vanishing moonlight-coloured atoms.
I am a bright wild poem.

Moments Like This

Mrs. Dalloway

She was not lovely—all green eyes
and a familiar swish of skirts—
but it was like God had bowed to her.

Lights and flowers blossomed round her.
She heard canaries whistling in secret.
Dogs took to her.
Even the darkness was exquisite.

She felt purified. She felt blessed.
This was a life!

Everything Is Clear
The Waves

Dancing alone, the ground slapping
against my soles

my blood billowing and rippling in me
my breath all quickness

I jump and shut my eyes and my pulse
seems to leap—it drums—

and I see this universe: the grass
the trees, my ribs

my very person. I am bright
a red gilt flower

and nothing is staid
nothing is settled.

I feel singled out—summoned
to triumph.

Cast Down

The Waves

I am tossed down into a huge uproar of people
the tumult extraordinary—

like the surge of the calling sea.
I become drawn in

with the swarms. I feel insignificant, lost
whirled asunder. In shock

fear resounds in my ears.
I stop and sit still one moment.

I will my sense of self to me
before it perishes.

Grasping my glass heart tightly
I emerge among the others

exultant as chaos.

Fortunes

The Waves

I am not beautiful, but I have never stopped
undressing like I am

summer heat or the storm-tinted scent of herbs.
I carry passion in my pinkish hands.

I follow love
and happiness to their red gate.

I like the cold smell of wet leaves on the ground
and the teething ferocity of the sea.

I like to see children dance
in fields—their nails bitten, their eyes content.

But more than anything—
more than laughter—I like to walk

through the long beautiful seasons
clutching at time

like it will let me be
old one day.

Composed

The Waves

This world is robbed of treasures—
it is unpacked boxes and callous
company—so I seek out the curious
the monumental: the white page
black ink, prayer. I have an identity—
I am here to write on wood desks
and wear my purple light
like a talisman.

Through to the Past
The Waves

Lost among rocks and crumpled ferns
the grass-green earth all mooning vagueness
I leap to the past—to the flicker
of firelight and love.

I see white petals move slowly in the wind
poets read with tears
in their black eyes

and yellow and pink fish with cold eyes
that ripple and follow me
are home in the sea.

This is where I laugh, I dance, I run.
I move and catch fire
and I do not dream
of the present.

Bound for Burning

The Waves

Shouting longing at parting friends
and gazing at coals feverishly like they are poetry—
that is the stab of love.

I am not whole now and I fill stealthily
with tears, untidiness, but no solidity.
I feel my familiars round me—

bringing me snatches of youth and astonishing love.
I fill with fire
and a little momentary pleasure.

I am mottled with desires
my life destroys.

Under the Waves
The Waves

I float beneath tremendous rippling lights—
gathering mist rolling over me
water in my ears
and yellow petals dissolving at the touch of the sea.

Then I sink and see nothing and everything
in the drum of innumerable waves:

holes in the face of a woman spread out on a ridge
a cowbind garland turns a hill grey
a white horse, mule like, stumbles over cliffs.

I settle on the sea bed
with spotted rippling flowers and a fleet of herring.

The end comes now—moonlight-coloured
and good—and I vanish:
a small darkened nothing.

Feverishly
The Waves

Here are remorseless beaks
that tap and tap and tap

my knuckles, brow, and the nape
of my neck.

My thin hard shell is separating
and my eyes fill
with warm tears. I am

overcome. I am not solid here—
not one and distinct—
and so I begin to doubt

who I am. I see the dead now.
I forget reality.

I feel so young and I cannot
find the wind.

The gold thread
in my soul is quivering.

I Cannot Return
The Waves

I fell to where water and the spinning
breeze and even the hours
are not indivisible.

I am crumbling here. Bits of me—
my thighs, fingers, feet—are slipping away.
I cannot clasp myself together.

I remember being one but now
I am only a tired half
woman sleeping side by side with bodies

cut in two. It seems I am
perceptible in this grey light—
I must still exist.

Depths

The Waves

I am unseeing now—black petals
are before my lidless eyes.

I hear the stirrings of green leaves
and the red swaying of flower after flower.

The tramplings of men and women
the tremblings of grey waters—

they shake me.
The earth is all tremors.

I go down into the hollows of the world
and I am alone

in the dark like pressed light—
my veins silver.

It Is Written
The Waves

Murder shuffles along. Anguished
Suicide sobs.
It is November and they are wind-bitten.
They are fasting.

For some fanatic reason all they want
now is sun and quiet and virtue.

Yet this is a broken world. A spirit
must fly on—one comes
into the storm then one goes out—
wings must beat.

So Violence and Death wait for reform
and regeneration.
They want the ordinary but
opulent. They want to not be unborn.

III

I Cannot Save Myself

The Waves

Now the kitchen door slams and dogs bark.
Now long hands shut a black book.
Now the others are crying. Now terror

stumbles in me. Now time—
green and wild—ticks on painfully.
Now the entire world

of stones and chalk and water is beginning
to look far away. Now it is my turn.
I am a looped figure on a blackboard

and I have begun to die.

Dying

The Waves

This is all new—changing from human to
some red firelit body.
Sleep and shadow are not safe now

but I force myself to look into the rising dark.
There, I sit in the shade of old yew trees
I only envy attachments

and poetry never again overflows in me.
Already—at this vision
and in my cowardice—I grow bitter.

The present is rippling
and darkening. I shut my eyes to it.
I hang over the edge.

Soon I will be a slip of history
a shadow of the past.
Myself—my life—unwritten.

On This Hill
The Waves

A pinch of wind stoops to brush
the top of a solitary carnation.
Red waters stumble towards
infinite depths. The old tree
is alone and I lie in my bed of bone
and dust. My wings have been
sliced. I have sunk on this height.
Beauty is dying.

This Bald Summer
The Waves

Life here is whispering and disguising our golden bodies.
We are the last men and women.

A monster stamps in the shadows. Dark clouds
bound over a wild sea
and a few shaggy ponies make off through the empty fields.

This present is emerging shocks—a tiger
chasing us and closing in.
We are the left behind.

Silence closes
heavily over every comfort.

Disembodied
The Waves

Petals float on these bright waters.
The man whose dreams have power fishes
the fathomless depths.
Early morning birds sing ephemeral
thoughts and the shore quivers
with childhood sounds. All is dreamlike
on this river but me.
I am a chained passerby—
the ghost of envy and bitterness.

With Anticipation
The Waves

This is an incredible place: oppressive
and red in its intensity.

Every moment in this abolished world
is unreal. Light glares its hostility

and metal flowers quiver with cold.
I do not have a normal body

here; I have lost the appearance of
somebody whole and only feel

a prickly blankness. This morbid place
sharpens my indifference—so I cut

people open with a white knife-blade
to see a flash of their wavering

being, to see them
undergo transformation. I know

now that there is extraordinary
pleasure in cruelty.

Brute

Mrs. Dalloway

This leaf-encumbered forest. This grubbing monster.
Stirring twigs. Her. Pain and scraped
pleasure—all hooves and power.
A moment of cracking. Nothing of beauty.
Her stirring hatred. Feel her spine and soul bend.
Hear her making her home in the depths.
Feel her rasped hurt
and quiver.

The Night Is Rapt
The Waves

I am roaming through the forest—plunging
through branches
pierced with arrows—and I feel uneasy.

The night is crowded with beasts and thorns.
All my senses are taut as the smell of violets
breaks over me and beckons.

I feel guilty and cold. Beneath the black boughs
I see moths rearing
among flashing yellow lights

and I hear a nightingale
sing. Blistered
by its red melody, I reel.

The darkness has broken me.
The crack in my body
is screaming.

Born Falling

The Waves

I am lost words and astonishing solitude.
I bring darkness everywhere I go

wreathing all in smoke
and boasting lies. I am nothing lovely—

no perfect being—but only
something fatal and weakening.

I cannot bear the pressure
of people or beauty and I enrage

whoever I see. My intensity will shatter
anything red and silver and loved.

I feel continually
remade into existence.

Separate

The Waves

I believe in horror—that fear persists.
Change leaps upon me—violent, tearing—
and I am in pieces.

One moment and I know I am not indivisible.
I do have a body but my face
is half-eaten—I have no beauty.
The shock is endless.

I press my hand to moonlight, see it foam
and draw back; I cannot force it
to merge with me.

I am bone and paper and green hours.
I am nothing. I grow
afraid because there is no end in view.

He Has Feasted
The Waves

The brute holds my story in his hands.
The savage ape-like thing
thrills over his desires for me. He purrs.

In dreams, he is surrounding me—
at dinner, on the streets, in a green garden—
he is there with his half-idiot gestures

and visceral controlling greed.
I become part of him.
He brindles and jibs. His hauntings

are red and smarting. He has brandished
his torch. His paw is on me.
He gobbles.

I clutch at what might have been.
The unborn shape of me.

I Will Not Go Under
The Waves

I sit alone between the beech trees
and wrap my matted hair in brambles.
I peer at agony inside the beech nuts
examine the raised wood—and take a saw to it.
The roots drink water from my fingers and die.
I shall sleep now and anguish
will not kiss me.

Always Him
The Waves

He talks of tortures and devastations—
and he is bored. His stories

sanction abandonment
and a certain extreme extravagance.

He seems to like lying
and insincerity—the vulture

that tears at grass and little boys
the appalling sentence

that tails off feebly. He makes us
all feel heavy and gaping.

But he is seductive
too. I feel his curious brutal power

then I feel foolish—
like a cricket dangling over teeth.

Now I no longer
think about lightness and laughter.

In Pursuit

The Waves

I am disinterested in perfection—I seek
only horror and deformity.

I always love the day's green envies
and grey bitterness
am done with everything silk.

I want a weak poem
novels about death and depravity
a slip of naked light.

I want fire and anguish and many
paper-knives.
I sit in cinders and rebuke the summer

breezes and dancing grasses.
They are eddying round me
ugly with virtue.

I tumble through the pages
of this world alone.

In Short
The Waves

I am yellow eyes
and rotted warmth.

I have turned
diamonds to leaves

and grass and stone
to ditch water.

I kiss the ground—
eat the insects.

I am the flecked light
the dead see

between the close
brown dust.

A Familiar Infinity
The Waves

The raw violence of death. A jungle of naked children
eating flesh. A man spearing
fish and dog. A sky full of holes.
It all only bores me.

When I drop asleep, the night strikes me with stars
and so my physical being is sometimes blazing.
I am like burnt paper.

I want to have desires again but I am
with the fallen now.

I am gifted at the ritual of inability—
and the truth is that I see
the satisfaction in it all.

This Is Us
The Waves

Now we tread on ferns that smell red
with age. Now we walk
among falling apples.

We wake the roses, the giant toad
the long sleeping earth.

There are the purple tree-tops.
There is the garden ringed with oak.

Now we have fallen
through the primeval undergrowth
and rot is strong in the air.

Now we are no longer unhappy.
We have never been
very human.

Brutally
The Waves

I am indistinguishable
from love—I have torn splendour

apart. Jealousy is in my eyes
in green depths.

I refresh hostility and diminish all
I perceive; I want you to hurt.

Rough hands, a shabby dress
I do not change

when I have the choice. I see you
trembling. I see your narrow

limits. You are unprotected: I am
raw fire, amorphous, huge.

I am immeasurable.

Stuck on This Page
The Waves

I let light turn to slabs of soot
slice ruthlessly at poetry and people
who choose to fear

spiders and drain-pipe and mud-stained waves—
I am marvellously corrupt.

The only things I like now are the jealousies
and antipathies
knocking gently on the door. I listen

to the delicate poet weep and chuckle:
this poem is torn
the myriad scraps irrelevant.

Horror and I are one in a faded
but infinite midnight.

Leave Us
The Waves

A festering swamp, a decomposing underworld
of vultures and maggots.

We crawl, curl up under a canopy of black leaves.
Everything is strange: the stars are purple
the flowers transparent.
This is our red rotting universe.

Here, there are giants and a worm
as thick as oak trees.

We killed light with an arrow.
Now we inhabit this fallen world.

Acknowledgements

Many thanks to the following journals, which first published a number of these poems:

The Account: 'I Cannot Save Myself' and 'Separate'
Aquifer: The Florida Review Online: 'Another Day'
The Believer: 'Ourselves'
Beloit Poetry Journal: 'Her Instinct'
Bennington Review: 'Without Sanctuary'
Blood Orange Review: 'The Playing-Field'
Bone Bouquet: 'Always Him' and 'I Cannot Return'
Boston Review: 'Brutally,' 'Stuck on This Page,' and 'What I Found'
DIAGRAM: 'She Admired the Dark' and 'Us'
Dreginald: 'Before the Wave,' 'In the Schoolroom,' 'Other People,' 'Remorselessly,' and 'Where They Sat'
Entropy: 'The Bird in My Heart Was Frightened'
Figure 1: 'This Is Us'
Fourth & Sycamore: 'The Mind Arches,' 'Phantom Weight,' and 'The Plunge Back'
Gulf Coast: 'The Night Is Rapt,' 'Rid of Effulgence,' and 'With Anticipation'
The Indianapolis Review: 'Everything Is Clear'
The Journal: 'Brim and Break'
Passages North: 'Born Falling' and 'Presence'
Phantom Drift: 'Leave Us'
Queen Mob's Teahouse: 'I Know Permanence'
RHINO: 'Fortunes'
Spillway: 'Never Eternally'

I'm grateful to so many individuals who were a part of making this collection a reality including Phillip Watts Brown (who introduced me to found poems), Maya Polan, Michael Wasson, Dahlia Seroussi, Heather Brown, Sally Parrish Blatt, Emily Dunford, Najma Khatri Newell, Kaely Horton, Matt Flanagan, and Ayelet Amittay (my best reader).

Thank you to my compassionate and so smart teachers Karen Holmberg and Jennifer Richter.

And an extended thanks to my family: Namira, Nishat, my mother Dillruba Islam, and my dad Mohamed Islam who is no longer with us but whose memory is very much alive.

Afterword

To write these poems, I select a paragraph from a Woolf novel—
The Waves or *Mrs. Dalloway*—and only use the words from that
paragraph to create a poem. I essentially write poems while
doing a word search using Virginia Woolf as source material.
I don't allow myself to repeat words, add words, or edit the
language for tense or any other consideration. These poems are
simultaneously defined by both Woolf's choices with language
as well as my own. They feel like an homage to this writer I
so admire as well as a way of authentically expressing my lived
experience.

Here is one excerpt from *The Waves*, which generated the poem
'Before the Wave':

'All **my** ships are white,' said Rhoda. '**I** do not want **red petals**
of **hollyhocks** or geranium. **I** want white petals that **float** when
I tip **the** basin up. I have **a** fleet now swimming from **shore** to
shore. I will drop a twig in as **a raft for a drowning sailor. I**
will **drop** a **stone** in **and see bubbles rise from the depths** of
the sea. Neville has **gone and** Susan has gone; Jinny **is** in the
kitchen garden picking currants **with** Louis perhaps. I have a
short time alone, while Miss Hudson spreads our copy-books
on the schoolroom table. I have a short space of **freedom.** I have
picked all **the fallen** petals and made them swim. I have put
raindrops in some. I will plant a **lighthouse** here, a head of
Sweet Alice. And **I** will now **rock** the **brown** basin from **side to
side** so that my **ships** may ride the **waves.** Some will founder.
Some will **dash** themselves **against the cliffs.** One sails alone.
That **is** my ship. It sails **into icy** caverns where the sea-bear **barks**
and stalactites swing **green** chains. **The waves rise**; their crests
curl; look at the lights on the mastheads. They have scattered,
they **have foundered**, all except **my** ship, which mounts **the
wave** and sweeps **before the gale and reaches the** islands where
the parrots chatter **and** the **creepers...**'

The Author

Nazifa Islam grew up in Novi, Michigan. Her poems and paintings have appeared in publications including *Boston Review, Blue Mesa Review, Gulf Coast, Entropy, The Believer,* and *Beloit Poetry Journal*; and her poetry collection *Searching for a Pulse* (2013) was published by Whitepoint Press.

She has long been fascinated by literature that is preoccupied with mental illness and the existential. Writers she admires, identifies with, and who are perpetually influencing her work include Sylvia Plath, Edgar Allan Poe, Virginia Woolf, and Fyodor Dostoevsky. She attempts to dissect, examine, and explore the bipolar experience through her writing. To that end, she has been working on a series of Sylvia Plath found poems in addition to her work with Woolf.

Nazifa earned her BA in English at the University of Michigan and her MFA at Oregon State University.

Lightning Source UK Ltd.
Milton Keynes UK
UKHW020937100222
398490UK00001B/87

9 781848 617841